for Preston! With love and gratitude.

Walk Through Paradise Backwards
poems by Trish Crapo

© 2004 Trish Crapo

Cover illustration—scratchboard drawing by Karen Gaudette
Frontispiece illustration—"Atop Blueberry Hill," pastel
by Gaal Shepherd

Grateful acknowledgment is made to the editors of the anthologies or journals in which these poems (or versions of them) first appeared: "The Conquerable World," Crossing Paths: An Anthology of Poems by Women, Mad River Press, Richmond, MA, 2002; "Moon Poem," Five Minute Pieces, Arms Library, Shelburne Falls, MA, 1998; "Ceremonial Breakage" and "Homing," *Sanctuary, The Magazine of the Massachusetts Audubon Society*, Lincoln, MA; "Surfacing" and "Gong," *Southern Poetry Review*, Savannah, Georgia.

The poem "Emily's Pins" owes a debt of scholarship to Marta Werner's excellent online essay, "The Flights of A821: Dearchiving the Proceedings of a Birdsong" and to Millicent Todd Bingham's introduction to the 1945 collection of Emily Dickinson's poems, Bolts of Melody, published by Harper & Brothers Publishers, New York.

Many thanks to Barry Sternlieb for his help and advice!

ISBN 0-9760643-0-8

Slate Roof: A Publishing Collective
15 Warwick Avenue
Northfield, MA 01360
www.SlateRoofPress.com

*for Kate & Liza,
my girls*

Cinderella, Differently

What if, when the messenger came,
Cinderella said, Oh that glass slipper—
I never cared about it! All night it pinched.
You ever try to dance in a glass shoe?
I would've preferred something flat, preferably soft.
Velvet, velour, kid glove leather, a little rabbit
turned inside out. I was glad to run down those stairs
when the clock struck. Glad to! If I'd had my wits
about me, I would've kicked off the *other* shoe!
It's gone anyway, like most happily-ever-after raptures—
the perfect man, the perfect marriage—
just when you think you're sitting pretty
in a golden carriage, you wake in the night,
put your hands out and realize what you're feeling
is the inside of a pumpkin.

Tell me, why should I marry this prince
just because I left my shoe at his house?
What I really want is to go barefoot.
I want to walk through paradise backwards
with my tongue hanging out, licking drops of sap
from the sides of trees, tasting grit, blood, clear water,
cloudy water, cracking open hives, tasting every kind of
honey there is. And I want a word for all this
so I can tell myself about it at midnight,
when I'm feeling low. I want a mantra
so big it doesn't fit in my mouth—a word like *lalange*,
which means, in Arabic, *the sound all of nature makes,
the language of birds.* I want a mantra that *is* birds—
whole flocks of them flung across the sky, miming
strange alphabets. Words like *om*, yeah, but how about
aya kallam, again Arabic, meaning, *Who knows what?*
And who does, messenger boy?
Who knows?

The Snake Speaks

Yes, I brought desire to paradise.
How else could humans enjoy it?
What did they want—indifferent bliss?

I loved Eve first, but she was
made of Adam. Bone of his bones,
she thought. He, her walking stick.
I envied their uprightness,
but I never mistook it for grace.
Grace is on the ground.
I run my belly over it daily.
And all night the earth's heat
is my heat, Eve's.
Blood of the body, the baby solid,
screaming in her arms, a woman knows
she's a tunnel the world moves through,
exchanging skins.

Adam forgot he was an animal—
I didn't have time to teach him everything!
How to love her. How to fuck without sin.
He still doesn't know the world is round,
that each trespass will bring him,
again, to temptation.

Me, I am the beginning.
I am new every time—
new, now.

The Conquerable World

Thomas Edison, nearly deaf,
taught his young sweetheart, Mina Miller,
to tap Morse Code on the back of his hand.
This was how, hurried dot by meticulous dash,
he pressed his request
on the inside of her wrist,
I love you. Will you marry me?
And Mina tapped back quickly, *Yes!*
though she already knew he loved
his own mind arcing toward
discovery more than anything.
But it was a new world,
a conquerable world—daily it revealed
long-kept secrets—and Mina
wanted to be part of it.

On their honeymoon, she helped him
try to shock a mussel shell open
by directing electricity through a trough of water.
The experiment failed—*Too bad,* Mina tapped.
In truth, she'd found herself
rooting for the mussel,
hoping this one small creature—
little more than a finger's length of flesh
inside its muddy double shield—could
withstand his curiosity.

Springtime in the Cathedral

We're out walking.
        My dog lolls in brown puddles
                until I catch up, then she rises and shakes,
                        spattering me.

Farther along, the road
        is festooned with manure—she kneels
                to the best piece, dips her shoulder
                        to receive its fragrant blessing.

We turn left off the road, head uphill
        through the muck and the bony
                blueberry bushes. I find footprints
                        from yesterday, softened in the sun

but still the right size, the right
        stride for me, my hips rolling
                in their sockets as I track myself
                        up to where the sun is stronger,

to where I can see Mt. Monadnock,
        where guy-wires of the radio tower
                sing a chord in a key
                        I never decipher.

But in the woods, I find someone has been cutting
        my trees—light spills
                onto stumps that smell of pine sap
                        and chain saw oil,

drag marks tear the ground down to leaf mold.
        Gone is all but the smallest brush.
              Of course, these are not my trees.
                      These are not my woods,

though I walk them.
        Still, this is where I stand.
              This is where the wind meets me,
                      where the leaves underfoot

make a sound like my name, and the sun
        throws rope ladders to the ground for me.
                I step onto a stump,
                      close my eyes.

Light enters me, splinters me, lovingly
        dismantles me, spit-shines me, stacks me,
                clatters me
                      to the forest floor.

You Don't Have to Take a Dog

You don't have to take a dog when you walk at night,
but it helps. Neighbors driving by
don't have to wonder
what tragic event has occurred to you—
whether you're trying to escape from your past
or your future, your husband, your kids,
or just the unwashed macaroni pot
hardening on the counter.
People who don't know you don't have to waste time
wondering who you are, though they might slow a bit,
on account of your dog.

The dog is oblivious.
That's part of her charm.
She trots on ahead of you,
sniffing for rabbits you'll never let her have.
She knows you'd spoil her chances, lose your cool
and shriek, *No!* right at the critical moment.
She loves you anyway. She's a dog.

You, on the other hand, are inescapably human.
Even if you could bring yourself
to charge into the underbrush after her,
baying at the top of your lungs, seeking,
maybe even finding, something vast and elemental,
some scrap of insight trapped and trembling
down a badger hole, there'd still be laundry
to do when you got home.

The moon's not full tonight but it's smiling anyway—
a lax, sideways smile—indulging you,
indulging your dog.
Cornstalks nudge one another as you pass.
All the decisions you've made lately,
all the tears you've cried or not cried,
and still this flat plain, this little piece of the world,
looks exactly the same.

The dog could have told you that.
She's waiting for you now, having left behind
the field's enticements to come onto the pavement
to find you. She sits, calm, watchful, wondering
how it is you can walk such a straight line
and still be so far back there.

Ceremonial Breakage

At Chaco Canyon, I spread my fingers,
comb the wind. I am a solid object, hours
are chunks of sun tumbled from the yellow cliffs,
the day a knot on a rope tying me
to the horizon. Drinking, I spill three drops.
Moments later, I'm not sure I believe in water.
If I stand still, the sky seeps into me,
if I run, lightning leaps, unburied, from the ground.

City upon city, and underfoot, time
fragments, pieces I toy with, laying this edge
to that, as if they are merely evidence of a pot
instead of a sure sign that I kneel here,
the ridges of my fingerprint catching in the hollows
of another woman's touch, my fingernail a stylus
releasing the song I know by heart,
that sang us both into being—the song
of the baby strapped to the carrying board,
clay gouged from the canyon floor, corn beat
with stones, arms opened to strangers,
turkey feathers plucked to make a blanket
for the dead. Two snakes mark the land
and in between, loneliness and obligation.
Brittle love, cumbersome water.
We lift the bowl. Let it drop.

Moon Poem
    for Linda

How did I lose track of the moon?
Living as I do in a place with no streetlights,
a place dark as the inside of my eyelids,
black as the bottom of a burnt pot.

You used to call me, and I'd run out to see the full moon,
a silver hubcap wobbling at the top of the hill, or waning,
a slice of melon ripe as any in the field.

Some nights I'd wake on my own,
my bed lit white, and wonder
what my Swedish ancestors feared
when they said, "Don't let the moon
shine on you while you're sleeping."

If I rise then, go into the kitchen for a glass of water,
the moon follows and I realize the danger—
I might wander off looking for something I lost,
something I loved, something that won't
come around again.

Call me melancholy.
I've been called worse.
The moon knows life leans
and fattens, one part joy,
two parts loss, and our job
is to make it come out even.

Maybe it was just a long month of cloud cover.
Maybe it was because your house burned down
and you moved. Or maybe I just forgot
how much I needed to see it—
pizza pan, squashed balloon,
thin edge of a dime,
spinning.

Return

What I felt first was the wedge of air at Lauderdale,
85 degrees and damp, shoving into the plane.
I remembered then that we were made of molecules—
my body, this metal container I traveled in, the sky—
there was barely room enough for all of us.
I remembered how to move and be still
at the same time. How not to sweat.

Outside baggage claim, I remembered the long and thin
fronds rustling, rattle of sea-grape leaves round
as cardboard bar coasters, and then the hot monotony
of the Florida Turnpike, big glittery bank buildings,
parking lots studded with palms.

Down in the Keys, my toes caressed the flat palmetto
grass, cool terrazo, gritty coral-rock paths.
My tongue curled toward the red star-shaped flowers
I used to dismember, teasing the stamen
from the stem for the drop of nectar. *Ixora*,
my friend who had stayed behind in Florida told me,
but I had never known the word for it, only the flavor.

By the beach, I knew these sun-streaked guys in flip-flops
renting inflatable rafts out of the backs of old Holsum
Bakery trucks—*Five bucks all day*—bicycle vendors peddling
banana-mango smoothies, frozen key lime pie on a stick.
I knew the Cuban women in house dresses
waiting for the kids to swim, biker chicks in halter-tops
and cut-offs, boxes of Marlboros and Daytona Cup
Special Edition Bic lighters in their butt pockets.
I knew the ganja-types, both white and black, in dreadlocks.

The cinnamon graham crackers I'd bought went soft
five minutes after I opened them. I put the past
in my mouth and I smiled, thinking, *This is the host
I was never allowed to take in Episcopal School*, but it wasn't 'til
later, halfway up the causeway, baptized, at last,
in the 93% humidity, that I really knew I was home.
All the car windows all the way down, water twenty shades
of aqua on either side of me, seagulls whirling away,
Janis on the radio, yowling, *You know you got it, child—
if it makes you feel good!*

Homing

I could throw armfuls of pigeons into the air,
watch to see if they remembered the point of release—
but how would I know which signified it: flight or return?

Migration begins when each bird is stricken
with uneasiness, a terror that spreads like a murmur
until the whole flock is knotted with a specific pain
nothing but flight will relieve. As a kid,
I ran breathless across the grass, scattering songbirds,
trying to get as close as I could to that startle,
that moment when fear lifted, became a broad shape
in the sky, headed home.

Father Piña Said

the sky was full of angels.
I did hear wings, sometimes voices,
but no one had poured water over me,
no one had taught me the prayers.
If God were to choose one of us
to receive him as we knelt, colored light
mottling us like minnows,
it wouldn't be me. Still,
the air was a room hollowed
by His breath, so when Father Piña
said, *Let us bow our heads,* I peeked.
Was it a joke or a miracle—the pigeon
fluttering in the rafters of the hot chapel,
mine the only eyes raised to see?

Surfacing

Eight or nine years old,
I stood on the dock
over the dark, slatted river,
waiting for the sea cow
to surface. I didn't know
the word *manatee*,
didn't know men
had mistaken her
for a mermaid.
I only knew that if I waited
she would arrive.

The river smelled
part bracken, part small-
engine oil and kissed the wall
with a sound so sexual
I was glad no one was near
to be embarrassed for.
A chubby kid, I was sure
my way into the world
wouldn't be through beauty.
And so, I had already begun
to run my fingers along
the fronts of words,
feeling for hinges.

The plastic bag of bread-ends
clammy in my hand,
sweat in my palm senseless
as hope—and then I saw her.
Ponderous, oblong, she wallowed
first, then spiraled up,

her face glamorous, human,
until she shed the glimmering
skin of water, broke the spell
with a comical snort.

I minded that she sloughed
her mystery off so easily,
though it comforted me too—
now I could give her bread
and watch her eat it.
But it was strange
to think she knew me.
Strange that she turned
from the soft weeds
along the bank—every day
about this time—nosed
into the current, pushing
toward me.

Back Then

Out in the yard, my sister and I
tore thread from century plants
to braid into bracelets, ate
chalky green bananas,
threw coconuts onto the sidewalk
to crack their hard, hairy skulls.

The world had begun to happen,
but not time. We would live
forever, sunburnt and pricker-stuck,
our promises written in blood. Not yet

would men or illness distinguish us,
our thoughts cleave us in two.
If she squeezed sour calamondines
into a potion, I drank it. When I jumped
from the fig tree, she jumped.

Chrysalis

If monarch butterflies are the souls of dead children,
do my two lost infants come to my garden every summer
to sip milkweed? Water babies, slippery possibilities,
your sisters are looking for you under the leaves.
They have built heaven in an old aquarium
and will stock it daily with what you need.
They want to see your striped bodies curl
and then harden, cupped inside your gold-spangled
green acorns until you darken with impossible wings.
Voracious journeyers, quivering appetites, hesitate
on their fingers before they release you: you are
all they know of Christ.

I Was Never One

of those matter-
of-fact mothers,
who tell their children
this is thus or what
to do. Though I knew
how to hold my babies
as soon as they were
handed to me, I could feel
how tremulous a life was.
This animal cradled on my heart, mine
for the naming, how was I to guess
at what it wanted?
Milk, yes. Love, yes. To lie on
me and sleep—yes, yes. But
what I wanted to know
about my babies stitched back
to what I'd been
when I was young—
to what I'd wanted—
and I couldn't remember that.
Sometimes, under my baby—
me a boulder, she a lion—
I'd feel our hearts beat
not as one, but stranger
still, as two hearts
pulsing through what
came between them—two
sets of ribs, two muscle walls, two
layers of skin. That I had pushed
my daughters from the dark
unknown of my own
body—I never
got over that.

The Size & The Weight of Home

I.
I can write these words, *Hawk flying over*
and a current of air passes through the room.
Put down the pen and sounds drop from my lips,
roll away across the floor.

Say to me, *I will love you forever*
and I'll stand, marooned, by the sofa.
Say, *The butter's in the cupboard*
and I am already spreading it, soft,
the way I like it, on my bread.

II.
Because communication is so difficult,
from now on we will let the natural world
speak for us in metaphors. When a tiger
enters the house, this means, *I am angry.*
A yellow jacket, slightly irritated.
Infiltrations of ants mean our lives
are being stolen away, piece by minuscule piece,
a fly buzzing around inside a juice glass means,
I feel trapped, I feel trapped, I feel trapped.

III.
I'm at the sink, doing dishes.
You read to me from the paper,
An eagle's nest weighs eight hundred pounds.
I put the plate in the rack, look out the window
to where snow is finally giving back the far fields,
exposing the bony slope where the Christmas trees
we planted as pencil seedlings thirteen years ago
have now outgrown all but the tallest rooms.

Like a Garden, Only Deeper

The year I turned forty, longing poured into me
like honey, only deeper. I wanted

things I didn't know the names for. I wanted
to drive 80 miles an hour down the interstate

applying lipstick, steering with my knee. Before me,
the horizon doubling away indefinitely, behind,

my tender perennials giving in to pigweed, pink-stalked,
bristly-seeded, edible—if you could stand the bitterness.

I wanted bitterness. I wanted a new life. I wanted
a young man to tattoo my name all over his body,

I wanted to wander around in the desert, half-starved
until I saw God.

But my husband sat down on the couch
and started watching home videos, one after the other,

hours of my children toddling toward me, offering
dandelions or already-chewed zwieback,

and my heart stuck. I saw how time had replaced
who I might be. Then,

the only possibility was to put my arms around
the expanding bones of my daughters and hang on

until, years from now, restless,
they struggle out of my life

into the wilderness of their own.

Sixteen

I knew you would never remain my ride-along
chimpanzee, my gap-toothed darling playing
chickens in the dug-out while the grown-ups
played softball. I flung you from my body
and now I wait—hand open
—for the arc of your return. Remember
the mint-green Soft-Serv stand I took you to
after the geese chased us to the car,
the bag of bread in your fist?
All the things I have to give you
are like that—fragile, meltable,
never quite enough to muffle
those beaks battering on the door.
Yesterday after we fought, my heart
rattled like a pie pan, trying to scare off
these years accumulating
between us. Stretching ahead,
your unknown life.

Owl
with all due respect to Emily Dickinson

I am getting to know the dailiness of grief,
the way sorrow swells the heart and stays there,
a feathered density that implies, but is not yet,
wisdom. You will be stronger for this,
the grasp of its talons assures me,
but I had not asked for strength.
I'd asked for happiness, I guess,
for love.

Each day I practice housing the owl,
transporting it in my rib cage from my sister's house
to the hospital, and back again. Six months ago,
I had not thought I would use the word *cancer*
or even *breast* so often. I had not yet learned
that hope is not a small feathered thing,
but a large one, with muscular wings
and, come nightfall, hungers of its own.

The Physics of Angels

I suspect the world remembers everything—
time and bones and words flung together
and me in it, suspecting. If we can believe
in photons—entities that possess movement
but not mass, and if the spirit, too
is made of light—then who am I to say
I haven't lived before—or you,
and thus this tenderness?
Who am I to doubt that grace
is elemental, like fire—or that souls
have no need of us, finally?

Gong

All that long year, grief
    hammered me thin
until I rang with a song
    I'd never heard.
It was not a dirge;
    it was a tune one
would hum oneself
    on the way to dying.
Under the panic
    clamor of my heart,
my bones reverberated
    an odd consolation.
I tried not to listen;
    I was afraid to die.
The dark of it scared me—
    the indefinability. I,
who must put a name
    to everything, how
would I know
    what I was?

Emily's Pins

Emily liked best the inside
of used envelopes; Emily liked
tiny scraps of stationery—pink,
yellow, blue—leaves torn
from old notebooks, drug-
and department store flyers,
chocolate bar wrappers, the cut-
off margins of newspapers, mildewed
magazine subscription blanks, the flip-
side of invitations, backs of brown-
paper bags. [Footnote: This poem
was written on a scrap of paper
twenty-one inches long
by three-quarters
of an inch wide.] Emily smothered
her scraps with words scrawled upside-
down, around the edge, wedged
between lines she had already written,
jabbed with dashes—tentative,
assertive—inflicting
their sharp points
of silence like pins. Emily
liked pins; she perforated
her scraps with possibility:
pinned and un-
pinned attachments, stanzas
stabbed together
and parted—hold
and release, love
and spurn. Emily
stacked alternate words three

and four high, like wood
to burn later. Emily wrote:
clogged [thronged] with music
like the Wheels [Decks]
of Birds. [Footnote:
This poem was written
on two, possibly three, sections
torn from an envelope,
pinned in the shape
of a bird.] Emily wanted
wings.

colophon

350 copies of
<u>Walk Through Paradise Backwards</u>
have been designed and published by
Slate Roof: A Publishing Collective, Northfield, MA.
Ten copies contain giclée prints signed by Gaal Shepherd.
Text is Baskerville, digitally printed on Mohawk Superfine
at Collective Copies, Florence, MA.
Cover is Wausau Royal Fiber, letterpress printed
at Swamp Press, Northfield, MA.

Trish Crapo grew up in Miami, Florida and now lives on an organic farm in Leyden, Massachusetts with her husband and two daughters. She writes poetry, fiction and essays.

Slate Roof is a not-for-profit collective committed to providing publishing opportunities for Franklin County poets. Slate Roof chapbooks are designed by the poets. When possible, all artwork is created by local artists.

Forthcoming chapbooks include works by

Jim Bell
Susan Middleton
Susie Patlove
Ed Rayher
Art Stein